Material Matters
Chemical Reactions

EXPRESS EDITION

Carol Baldwin

Raintree

Chicago, Illinois

For information, address the publishers:
Raintree, 100 N. LaSalle, Suite 1200, Chicago, IL 60602

Printed and bound in China
10 09 08 07
10 9 8 7 6 5 4 3 2

Library of Congress Cataloging-in-Publication Data

Cataloging-in-publication data is available at the Library of Congress

Baldwin, Carol, 1943-
  Chemical reactions / Carol Baldwin.
    p. cm. -- (Material matters)
  Includes bibliographical references and index.
  ISBN 1-4109-1674-X (library binding-hardcover) -- ISBN 1-4109-1681-2 (pbk.)
  ISBN 978-1-4109-1674-7 (library binding-hardcover) -- ISBN 978-1-4109-1681-5 (pbk.)
  1. Chemical reactions--Juvenile literature. 2. Strength of materials--Juvenile literature. [1. Chemical reactions. 2. Strength of materials.] I. Title. II. Series: Baldwin, Carol, 1943- Material matters.
  QD501.B2342 2005
  541'.39--dc22

This leveled text is a version of Freestyle: Material Matters: Chemical Reactions.

Acknowledgments
Page **33** right, Andrew Lambert; **13**, Chris Honeywell; **39**, Gareth Boden; **27**, Trevor Clifford; **4**, Tudor Photography; **20**, Tudor Photography; **35**, Tudor Photography; **41**, Tudor Photography; **9** right, Art Directors & Trip; **14**, Art Directors & Trip; **38**, Art Directors & Trip; **40** right, Art Directors & Trip/ T Freeman; **42**, Art Directors & Trip/A Lambert; **37**, Art Directors & Trip/Australia Picture Library; **31**, Art Directors & Trip/C Kapolka; **17**, Art Directors & Trip/C Smedley; **24** right, Associated Press; **32**, Associated Press; **4–5**, Corbis; **8**, Corbis; **15**, Corbis; **25**, Corbis; **36–37**, Corbis; **40** left, Corbis; **10–11**, Corbis/C O'Rear; **16**, Corbis/Duomo; **28**, Corbis/E Whiting; **22**, Corbis/ G Rowell; **23**, Corbis/MacFadden Publishing; **12–13**, Corbis/O Franken; **22–23**, Corbis/P Turnley; **28–29**, Corbis/R Gehman; **10**, Corbis/R Krist; **11**, Corbis/T Lang; **43**, Corbis/T Stewart; **18**, Digital Vision; **34–35**, FLPA/ Gerard Lacz; **14–15**, FLPA/L Lewis; **20–21**, FLPA/R Tidman; **19**, FLPA/W Meinderts; **12**, Foodpix; **5** bottom, Forensic Alliance; **42–43**, Forensic Alliance; **5** top, NASA/ Kennedy Space Center; **18–19**, NASA/ Kennedy Space Center; **29**, NASA/Jet Propulsion Laboratory; **6–7**, Photodisc; **7**, Photodisc; **6**, Robert Harding; **30**, Science Photo Library/ Charles D Winters; **30–31**, Science Photo Library/ Charles D Winters; **38–39**, Science Photo Library/ Michael Abbey; **9** left, Science Photo Library/Alex Bartel; **21**, Science Photo Library/CNRI; **26**, Science Photo Library/D Parker; **26–27**, Science Photo Library/D Spears; **24** left, Science Photo Library/M Chillmaid; **34**, Science Photo Library/P Ryan/Scripps; **16–17**, Science Photo Library/P Scoones; **5** middle, T.Waltham/Geophotos; **36**, T.Waltham/Geophotos; **45**, T.Waltham/Geophotos; **33** left, TDG Nexus/Mark Perry/Simon Peachey; **44**, TDG Nexus/ Mark Perry/Simon Peachey -

Cover photograph of a reaction taking place in a test tube reproduced with permission of Corbis/Lester Lefkowitz

Every effort has been made to contact copyright holders of any material reproduced in this book. Any omissions will be rectified in subsequent printings if notice is given to the publishers.

Contents

Any words appearing in the text in bold, **like this**, are explained in the Glossary. You can also look for some of them in the Word bank at the bottom of each page.

Explosion!

Different colors

The sparks in fireworks shoot out in all sorts of colors. These come from different chemicals. Yellow sparks come from sodium. A bright, white color comes from magnesium. Green sparks come from copper.

A firework shoots high into the sky. Boom! The firework explodes. A splash of red spreads across the sky. A few seconds later, another firework goes off. A huge ball of bright white sparks lights up the sky. Next there are sizzling, spinning wheels of green. Lights, colors, and sounds are all part of firework displays. They show that changes are taking place in the fireworks.

Fireworks contain explosive chemicals. They are very dangerous.

Changes all around us

Materials around us change all the time. Some changes take less than a second. Exploding fireworks are like this. Other changes take longer. The rusting of a car takes many years.

When materials change, they often produce one or more new materials. If this happens, a **chemical reaction** has taken place. This book tells you all about chemical reactions.

Fireworks give brilliant displays of light and noise. They are a big part in celebrations around the world.

Find out later ...

... how chemical reactions power the Space Shuttle.

... how caves form.

... how police use chemical reactions.

Matter

Everything around us is made up of **matter**. The food we eat and the clothes we wear are matter. All matter is made up of **atoms**. Atoms are tiny **particles** that make up everything. But not all atoms are alike.

Elements

There are over a hundred **elements**. An element is made from just one kind of atom. Different elements are made from different atoms. Silver is an element. So are carbon and oxygen.

What is matter?
This flash of lightning is not matter. It is electrical **energy**. But the air it passes through is matter.

Water is a compound. It is made of the elements hydrogen and oxygen.

Word bank   matter anything that takes up space and has mass

Compounds

Compounds are made up of atoms of more than one element. Carbon dioxide is a compound. It is made of carbon and oxygen atoms. There is a set number of each kind of atom in a compound. Carbon dioxide has two oxygen atoms for each carbon atom.

The atoms in a compound join together in special ways. They are held together tightly. You can break compounds into simpler materials. But this is often hard to do.

Mixtures

The topping on this pizza is a **mixture**. It contains sauce, cheese, and other toppings. But they are not joined together. They can be separated easily.

You can describe **matter** by its features. These are called **properties**. There are two main types of properties. One kind is physical. The other kind is chemical.

Physical properties

You can find out the **physical properties** of a material easily. You do not need to change it. You can usually tell physical properties by looking or measuring. Color and **state of matter** are physical properties. For example, lemon juice is yellow. It is in a liquid state. These are all physical properties.

Cars are different sizes, shapes, and colors. These are physical properties of cars.

Chemical properties

Chemical properties tell us how a material will **react** with something else. Wood is able to burn in air. This is a chemical property. It is useful because it gives us heat and light.

If you leave your bicycle outdoors, it will rust in time. Rust forms when iron reacts with oxygen and **water vapor** in the air. This is a chemical property of iron. A material has to change before you can find out its chemical properties.

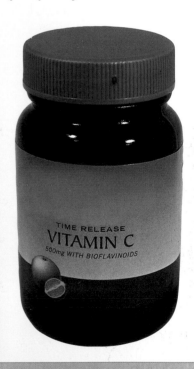

This is a pile of scrap material. The iron is attracted to this huge magnet. This is a useful physical property for separating iron.

Changing Matter

A large bell
To make a bell, melted metal is poured into a mold. The metal then sets into a solid. A large bell has to cool very slowly to prevent the metal from cracking.

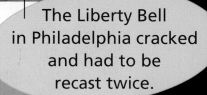

The Liberty Bell in Philadelphia cracked and had to be recast twice.

Physical changes
An artist carves wood to make a sculpture. He changes its shape, but he does not change the wood. This is a **physical change**.

Matter changes from solid to liquid, from liquid to gas, and back again. These are changes in **state of matter**.

When liquid water changes to solid ice in a freezer, it is still water. This is a physical change.

This is melted copper. When it cools, it will turn back into a solid. This is a physical change.

Word bank   physical change change in how something looks, not in what makes it up

Chemical changes

When wood burns in a fireplace, it changes. The wood joins with oxygen in the air. Ash, **water vapor**, and carbon dioxide gas are formed. Ash is a soft, gray material. Water vapor and carbon dioxide are gases with no smell or color. These new materials look and act different from the wood. A chemical change, or a **chemical reaction**, has taken place.

A chemical reaction is a change that results in new materials.

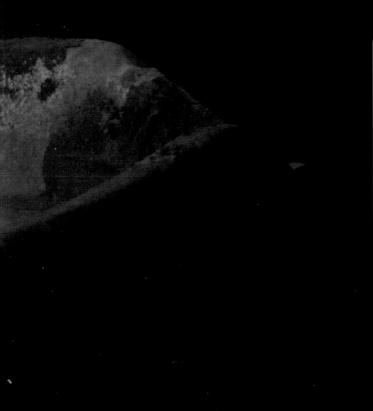

Batteries
There are chemical changes going on in this flashlight's battery. These changes make electricity. The bulb lights up.

chemical reaction change that produces one or more new materials

Baking cakes

When you bake a cake a chemical reaction happens. The ingredients **react** together. They make carbon dioxide gas. As the cake bakes, bubbles of carbon dioxide rise through the cake mix.

Clues to chemical changes

A **chemical reaction** is taking place if there is a fire. Other chemical changes give off **energy** without fire. The energy can be heat, light, sound, or electricity. Giving off energy is a sign of chemical change.

Other clues that a chemical reaction has taken place are:

- bubbles of gas in a liquid. This happens when sodium bicarbonate is placed in vinegar.

- a colour change. For example, when sugar is heated for a long time, it changes from a brown liquid to a black solid.

This pancake has bubbles on its surface. They are a clue that a chemical reaction has taken place.

Gases escape into the air when wood burns. So burning wood gets lighter.

energy ability to do work. Energy is transferred whenever something happens.

Keeping mass

When a chemical reaction takes place, new materials are formed. But the **mass** stays the same. The mass of something is the amount of **matter** it has. There are still the same number of **atoms**. The atoms are just rearranged.

In chemical reactions, no matter is lost and none is made. For example, iron and oxygen join together to form iron **oxide**. If you add the mass of the iron to the mass of the oxygen, you find that it is the same as the mass of the iron oxide.

Burning candles

A candle gets smaller as it burns. It looks as if it loses mass. But as it burns, it gives off gases. The mass of the gases would be the same as the mass of the missing candle.

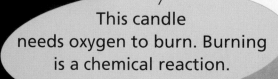

This candle needs oxygen to burn. Burning is a chemical reaction.

Describing chemical reactions

You can describe **chemical reactions** by using **word equations**. In a word equation, the names of the **reactants** are on the left. The names of the **products** are on the right. An arrow separates the reactants from the products. It means "produces." The arrow points from the reactants to the products.

Hydrogen **reacts** with oxygen to form water. The word equation for this reaction is:

$$hydrogen + oxygen \rightarrow water$$

Kitchen reaction

You can mix vinegar and baking soda together. These reactants produce water and sodium ethanoate. The bubbles are carbon dioxide gas.

The copper of this statue reacts with carbon dioxide and **water vapor** in the air. It forms a layer of green copper carbonate.

reactant　material that reacts with another material during a chemical reaction

Chemical symbols

There is a short way of writing the names of **elements**. We use **chemical symbols**. Symbols can be one or two letters. The first letter is always a capital letter. The second letter is always lower case. For example, the symbol for magnesium is Mg, not MG, and the symbol for sodium is Na, not NA.

Common chemical symbols
- Hydrogen   H
- Gold   Au
- Sodium   Na
- Copper   Cu
- Iron   Fe
- Sulfur   S
- Carbon   C

This is table salt, or sodium chloride, Na Cl. It is made from sodium, Na, and chlorine, Cl.

Chemical formulas

You can use **chemical symbols** to write **formulas**. A formula shows how **atoms** are joined and how many. Oxygen has the formula O_2. The O stands for oxygen. The "2" is written below the line. This tells us that there are two **atoms** of oxygen joined together.

A number is often written on the line. Then it refers to atoms or **molecules** that are not joined. Two atoms of carbon that are not joined are written as 2C.

Formulas of compounds

Formulas are used to write the names of **compounds**, too. The formula for carbon dioxide is CO_2. This means that a carbon dioxide molecule has one carbon atom and two oxygen atoms.

Chlorine

Chlorine **reacts** with most other **elements**. When hot sodium is put into a jar of chlorine gas, sodium chloride is formed. There is so much heat the sodium burns in the chlorine.

Chlorine is added to swimming pools. It kills bacteria.

formula symbols and numbers used to show how atoms are joined

The formula for water is H_2O. This means a molecule of water has two hydrogen atoms joined to one oxygen atom.

Aluminum is used to make these airplane wings.

This is a welding torch. It is being used under water. It uses the reaction between hydrogen, H_2, and oxygen, O_2, to produce extreme heat.

Aluminum
Aluminum is mostly found joined to oxygen in Earth's crust. It is in the compound, aluminum oxide. A lot of energy is needed to produce pure aluminum. This makes it expensive.

molecule two or more atoms held together by chemical bonds

Kinds of Chemical Reactions

"Putting together" reactions

Two or more **elements** or **compounds** often join together. They form one new compound. This type of reaction is called a **synthesis reaction**. In synthesis reactions, there is only one **product**. The reaction between iron and sulfur is like this. They join together to form the compound iron sulfide.

"Breaking apart" reactions

In some reactions, a compound is broken apart. Then simpler materials are made. This type of reaction is called a **decomposition reaction**. A compound can break apart to form two elements. Water is made up of two hydrogen atoms and one oxygen atom. When water is split, hydrogen and oxygen are formed.

Acid in the air

Acid rain occurs when sulphur and nitrogen oxides join with water in the air, forming **acids**. The acids fall to Earth as **acid rain** or snow.

Acid rain flows into streams or ponds. There it can kill plants, frogs, fish, and snails.

Word bank   acid rain   rain containing nitric acid and sulfuric acid

A single compound can break up into two other compounds. The formula for copper carbonate is $CuCO_3$. When copper carbonate is heated it breaks apart. It forms two compounds:

• copper oxide, CuO

• carbon dioxide, CO_2.

Decomposers
Some living things are called **decomposers**. Molds and mushrooms are examples of these. They break apart the compounds in dead plants, animals, and waste. The simpler materials can be used again.

This beefsteak fungus gets **energy** by breaking down compounds in plant waste.

The reaction between hydrogen and oxygen produces huge amounts of **energy**. This powered the lift-off of the Space Shuttle.

Button batteries

Button batteries are small. They are used to power watches and hearing aids. A displacement reaction takes place in button batteries. This releases the **energy**.

Displacement reactions

In a simple **displacement reaction** you have one **element** on its own and a **compound**. The element pushes out one of the elements in the compound. It takes its place. This is a simple **displacement reaction**.

Ironworkers set up a simple displacement reaction to make iron. Much of our iron comes from iron **oxide**. Iron oxide is made of iron and oxygen. Iron oxide reacts with carbon. The carbon "pushes out" the oxygen, making carbon dioxide. This leaves iron on its own.

Large ships have magnesium bars in their iron hulls. The magnesium stops the iron hull from rusting in the salt water. This happens because of a displacement reaction.

OCEAN PRINCESS
NASSAU

Other displacement reactions

Displacement reactions can happen between two compounds. The elements in the two compounds switch places.

This happens when sodium chloride reacts with silver nitrate. First, both compounds are **dissolved** in water. When they are mixed, a white solid appears. This is silver chloride. Sodium nitrate is also formed. But that stays dissolved in the water. So you cannot see it. Sodium chloride and silver nitrate have "swapped partners." The sodium is now "partnered" with nitrate and silver has "teamed up" with chloride.

Looking inside
Barium sulfate shows up in X-rays. A person who is ill is given a barium sulfate **mixture** to drink. X-ray photographs are taken. They show doctors what the **intestine** looks like.

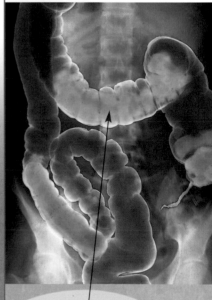

Barium sulfate is a solid. It is made in a displacement reaction.

Reactions and Energy

Exothermic reactions

Exothermic reactions are **chemical reactions** that give off energy. When people go camping, they often light a fire. The wood gives off heat **energy** when it burns. It also gives off light energy.

When something burns, it gives off heat and light energy. There is an exothermic reaction going on.

Rusting

Rusting is an exothermic reaction. But if you touch a rusting car, it does not feel hot. This is because rusting happens very slowly.

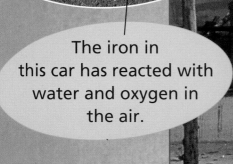

The iron in this car has reacted with water and oxygen in the air.

When a building catches fire, it can get so hot that the steel beams melt.

WIN $10,000
DOWN ON A NEW CAR!

Word bank　exothermic reaction　reaction that gives off energy, usually in the form of heat and light

Endothermic reactions

Some chemical reactions need energy all the time to keep them going. As soon as there is no energy, they stop. They are called **endothermic reactions**. Carrots cook only when they are in hot water. If the carrots are put into cold water, they stop cooking.

We can split water into hydrogen and oxygen. But this reaction needs energy, or it will stop. You have to pass electricity through the water. This process is called **electrolysis**.

In the limelight

Calcium oxide is often called **lime**. If lime gets very hot, it gives out a bluish-white light. This light was once used to light theater stages.

This stage is lit by electricity.

Reaction Rates

Fresh or sour

Keep milk cool. It stays fresh longer. Chemical reactions make milk sour. These happen more slowly at low temperatures.

Wood burns quickly, and iron rusts slowly. These **chemical reactions** take different lengths of time. They have different rates. The **reaction rate** tells us how fast a reaction happens. There are two ways to measure a reaction rate. You can measure how quickly one of the **reactants** disappears. Or you can measure the time it takes for one of the **products** to form.

Temperature

Most chemical reactions speed up when the temperature increases. A cake will bake faster in a hot oven than in a cooler oven.

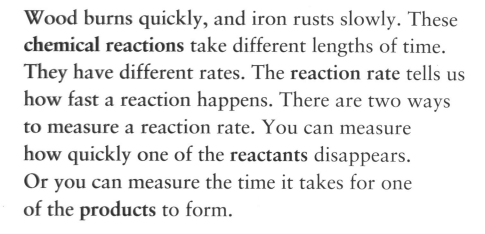

This milk is sour. The liquid is called whey, and the fatty solids are called curds.

The grain stored in these silos has caught fire. The dust from the grain burns so fast it can cause explosions.

reaction rate measure of how fast a reaction happens

Concentration

The amount of a material in a certain space is the **concentration**. When the concentration is high, the **particles** are close together. They are more likely to bump into each other. A high concentration will speed up a reaction.

Particle size

Reactant particles can be different sizes. This affects the speed of a reaction. Smaller particles react faster. It is easier to start a fire with small twigs than big logs.

Flour
Flour particles are very tiny. They have a huge **surface area**. They are more likely to touch each other. This means they burn instantly.

In 1965, an explosion at this flour mill in London killed four people.

Catalysts

Chemical reactions can be too slow to be useful. Then people use **catalysts**. These speed up reactions. But catalysts do not take part in reactions. Catalysts do not change or get used up. The amount of catalyst at the end of the reaction is the same as at the start.

Seeing clearly

Contact lens cleaning solution contains enzymes. Enzymes speed up the reactions that break down the dirt. The amount of enzymes is the same after cleaning the lenses as before.

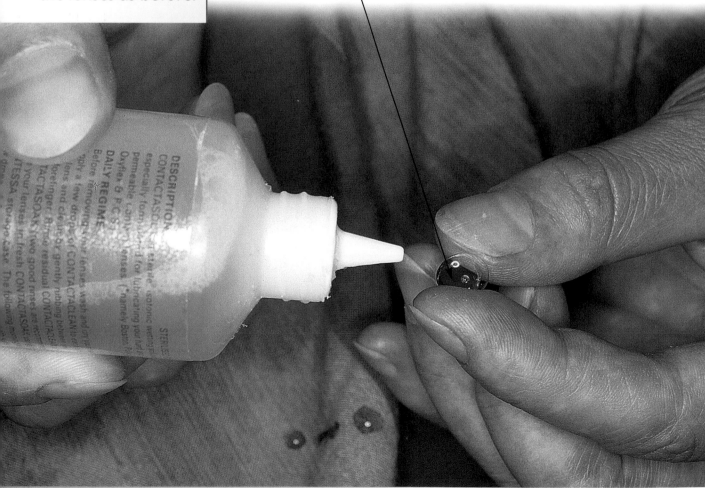

Dirt collects on contact lenses, and they get cloudy. People need to clean them.

catalyst material that speeds up a reaction without being used up

Enzymes

All living things use catalysts. These are called **enzymes**. Spiders eat insects for food. First, the spider bites the insect. Then it pours enzymes into the insect's body. The enzymes speed up the breakdown of the insect's body. It turns into soft goo, and the spider sucks it up.

Inhibitors

Sometimes foods and medicines spoil too quickly. This is because chemical reactions happen too fast. They need to be slowed down. People use **inhibitors** to do this.

Brown apples
Chopped apples react with oxygen in the air. This makes them turn brown. You can add lemon juice to the apples as soon as they are cut. This slows down, or inhibits, this reaction.

This spider is using enzymes to help break down its victim's body.

enzyme material that speeds up reactions in living things without being changed

More Chemical Reactions

Oxidation
Many materials **react** with oxygen. This is called **oxidation**.

Fast reactions with oxygen
Materials can react with oxygen very quickly. This is called burning. Paper, candles, and logs all burn because they react with oxygen fast.

Burning is useful. It gives off heat and light **energy**. We burn **fuel** to heat our homes and to run cars. Burning can also be harmful—fires can kill.

Burning without oxygen
Carbon monoxide can kill you. It is a gas with no color or smell. When fuel burns and there is not enough oxygen, carbon monoxide forms.

This stove uses wood as a fuel. This can produce carbon monoxide if there is not enough oxygen.

oxidation reaction when a material joins up with oxygen

Slow reactions with oxygen

Materials can also react with oxygen slowly. This is called slow oxidation. Rusting is slow oxidation. Rust forms slowly on iron and steel in cars and bridges. Rust is the **compound** iron **oxide**. Iron oxide is made up of iron and oxygen.

Reduction

Some reactions remove oxygen from a material. This is called **reduction**. Reduction is the opposite of oxidation. Reduction reactions are useful. Reduction makes zinc oxide into zinc and oxygen.

Rusty rocks
Some rocks have iron in them. The iron in them reacts with the oxygen in air. Iron oxide, or rust, forms. The rocks become red or orange in color.

Forest fires kill plants and animals.

reduction   reaction that happens when oxygen is removed from a material

Reactivity series

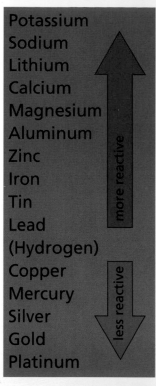

Potassium
Sodium
Lithium
Calcium
Magnesium
Aluminum
Zinc
Iron
Tin
Lead
(Hydrogen)
Copper
Mercury
Silver
Gold
Platinum

more reactive

less reactive

Metals and water

Most metals do not **react** with water. But there are some metals that react violently. These are lithium, sodium, potassium, rubidium, and caesium. Other metals will react with water, but more slowly. These are calcium, strontium, and barium. Magnesium reacts very slowly with cold water.

Metals and acids

Only some metals react with **acids**. The **reactivity series** chart on the left tells us the metals that will do this. The metals listed above hydrogen react with acid. The metals listed below hydrogen do not react with acid.

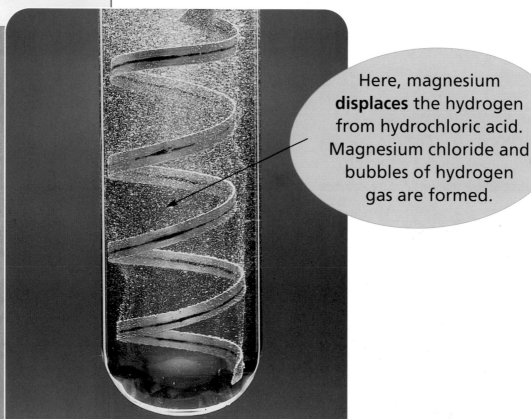

Here, magnesium **displaces** the hydrogen from hydrochloric acid. Magnesium chloride and bubbles of hydrogen gas are formed.

reactivity series materials listed by how easily they react with other materials

Metals and other compounds

During a **chemical reaction**, some metals push out other metals in a **compound**. You can use the chart, opposite, to tell you the metals that will do this.

For example, in the reaction between iron and copper sulfate, the iron pushes out the copper. Iron sulfate and copper are formed. This is because iron is more reactive than copper.

Mending tracks
Aluminum reacts with iron oxide. The **products** are aluminum oxide and iron. This reaction produces huge amounts of heat. This melts the iron. The melted iron is used to mend railroad tracks.

This potassium is reacting violently with water. Potassium must be stored under oil to keep it away from water.

Acid everywhere

In 1996, a train in Colorado derailed, or fell off the tracks. It was carrying a strong acid. The acid spilled across a highway. People used **soda ash** and **lime** to clean up the spill. These bases neutralized the acid.

Neutralization reactions

The reaction between an **acid** and a **base** is called **neutralization**. A **neutral** material is not an acid and it is not a base. Water is a neutral material. This type of reaction forms water and a **salt**. This is shown below.

acid + base ⟶ salt + water

For example hydrochloric acid reacts with the base, sodium **hydroxide**. Water and the salt, sodium chloride, form. Sodium chloride is table salt.

Special suits protect people who clean up acid spills.

base chemical that neutralizes acids. Metal oxides and metal hydroxides are bases.

Salts

Sodium chloride is the **compound** we call salt.
Sodium chloride is used to make many things.
These include ice cream, rubber, and soap.
But this is just one of many salts.

A salt is made when an acid reacts with a base.
Different acids and bases form different salts.

Other acid reactions
Limestone, marble, and chalk react with acids. They produce bubbles of carbon dioxide gas.

This tanker is carrying sodium hydroxide. The numbers on the label tell us this. The label also shows us the possible dangers.

2R
1824
CORROSIVE
01928 580588

Scientists use this acid reaction to test for carbonate rock.

carbonate compound that contains carbon, oxygen, and another element

33

Reactions in Nature

Food without light

Sunlight is needed to make food. But sunlight cannot reach the deep parts of the ocean. There, **bacteria** make food using sulfur **compounds**. This happens where hot water spurts out of the sea floor.

Tube worms live in deep seas. They live on bacteria.

Eucalyptus trees make their own food. This koala has to eat the leaves to get energy.

respiration chemical reaction in which glucose and oxygen react to form carbon dioxide and water, releasing energy

Photosynthesis

Plants can make their own food. This process is called **photosynthesis**. Plants take in carbon dioxide gas through their leaves. Plants take in water from the soil through their roots. Carbon dioxide and water **react** together, using light **energy** from the Sun. A sugar, called **glucose**, and oxygen are produced.

Respiration

All living things need energy to grow and live. They use a process called **respiration**. Respiration is a **chemical reaction** between the sugar (glucose) and oxygen. Plants make their own glucose. Animals eat plants and other animals to get glucose. Animals breathe in oxygen. Plants take in oxygen through tiny pores. In respiration glucose and oxygen react together. Respiration produces energy.

Brown iodine turns blue-black if starch is present.

Breaking down food

Foods like bread contain **starch**. Starch is made of glucose. When we chew, we make **saliva**. Saliva breaks down starch into glucose.

photosynthesis reaction between carbon dioxide and water, using light energy, to form glucose and oxygen

Acids and carbonates

Carbonates are **compounds** that contain carbon and oxygen. **Acids react** with carbonates. Caves form when an acid reacts with carbonate rocks.

How caves form

The reason caves form in the first place is rain. Rainwater joins with carbon dioxide in the air. It makes a weak acid, called carbonic acid. This acid reacts with calcium carbonate rocks, like limestone. Caves and tunnels are made as the acid eats through the rock.

Lechuguilla Cave

This cave is in New Mexico. It formed when acid ate through the limestone underground.

Lechuguilla Cave is a maze of tunnels and caves.

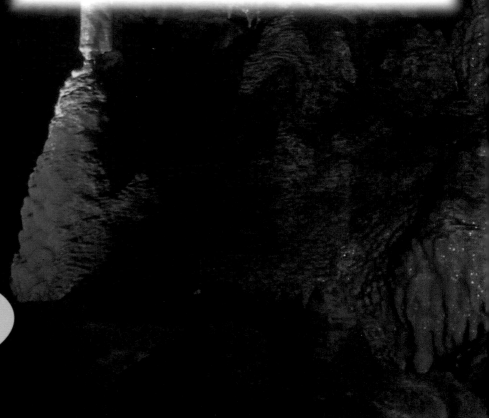

acid rain rain containing nitric acid and sulfuric acid

Acid rain

Burning **fossil fuels**, like coal, gas, and oil, cause **acid rain**. Sulfur dioxide gas and nitrogen **oxide** gases combine with the **water vapor** in the air. This forms strong acids. Acid rain falls to Earth.

Acid rain reacts with marble and limestone. This damages many buildings and statues. Acid rain kills some kinds of trees. It also makes soils acidic, and some plants cannot grow in them.

Neutralizing acidic lakes

Most living things die in acidic water. But you can treat it with powdered limestone. The limestone **neutralizes** the acid in the water. Then plants and animals can live in the water again.

Airplanes, helicopters, and boats are used to spread limestone on acidic lakes.

fossil fuel fuel formed from the remains of plants and animals that lived millions of years ago; coal, oil, and gas are fossil fuels

Amazing Reactions

Nonstick cookware

Cooking eggs is easy in this frying pan. It has a nonstick surface. The slippery material used on the surface was found by accident. This was a surprise **chemical reaction**!

Baking bread

To make bread "rise," people mix **yeast** into bread dough. Yeast **reacts** with the sugar in wheat flour. The reaction forms carbon dioxide gas and alcohol. The gas makes many little bubbles. These cause the bread dough to rise.

The heat from the oven drives off the carbon dioxide and the alcohol. But tiny holes are left in the bread. This is where the carbon dioxide gas bubbles were formed.

This photo shows tiny yeast cells. It was taken through a microscope.

Word bank   yeast type of fungus used to make bread rise

Body enzymes

Our bodies need food for growth and repair. But food has to be broken down into simple chemicals. Then our bodies can use the food. This process is called **digestion**.

Digestion is a whole series of **chemical reactions**. **Enzymes** speed up the chemical reactions. Food is broken down in the mouth, the stomach, and the small intestine.

Lactose intolerance

Some people do not have the enzyme lactase. Lactase breaks down the sugar lactose found in milk. These people feel sick when they drink milk.

Milk, like this, makes some people ill.

Reactions in your mouth

Bacteria in our mouths produce **acids**. The acid reacts with the surface of the teeth. Then bacteria and acid attack the inside of the teeth, too.

Using hand warmers

Hand warmers are small pouches. They contain iron powder and **catalysts**. When you shake the pouch, it mixes the iron powder with air. The iron powder **reacts** with oxygen in the air to form rust. This reaction gives off heat. The catalysts speed up the reaction. This means heat is given off much faster than normal rusting.

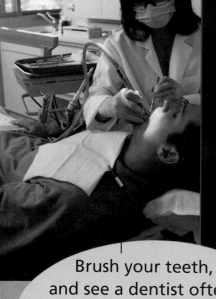

Brush your teeth, and see a dentist often! This keeps teeth free of acid-producing bacteria.

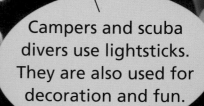

Campers and scuba divers use lightsticks. They are also used for decoration and fun.

catalyst material that speeds up a reaction without being used up

Using lightsticks

When you bend a lightstick, the chemicals inside mix. As soon as the chemicals touch each other, they react. The reaction is **exothermic**. It produces light **energy**. This causes the lightstick to glow.

In cold conditions, the reaction is slower. The lightstick glows less, but it lasts longer. In warm conditions, the reaction is faster. The lightstick glows brighter, but for a shorter time.

Hard water
Water is "hard" because it has **salts dissolved** in it. The salts react with soap to form soap scum. Soap scum sticks to the sides of bathtubs.

bacteria living things so small you need a microscope to see them

Hospital science

Doctors use chemical tests. These find out why a person is ill. The tests measure chemicals in the blood. One test measures how much **glucose** is in the blood. Glucose is a type of sugar. If the glucose level is high, a person might have **diabetes**. People with diabetes sometimes have too much sugar in their blood.

There are many other tests to check a person's health. They all depend on **chemical reactions**.

Daily blood tests
People with diabetes have to check the glucose in their blood. The tests they use are all reactions between glucose and other chemicals.

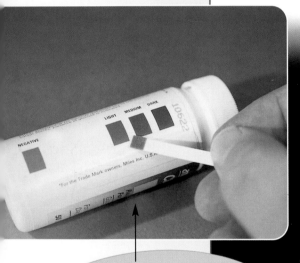

Some glucose tests have a color chart. The color of the test strip shows the person's glucose level.

Forensic science

Police use chemical tests to help solve crimes. Luminol is one chemical police use. This helps them look for traces of blood. Police mix luminol with hydrogen peroxide. This usually produces a very slow **exothermic** reaction. In the dark, the police would see a faint blue-green glow after a while.

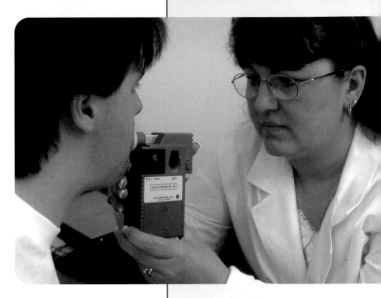

But if blood is there, the reaction happens much quicker. The police see a bright glow in seconds.

Take a deep breath and blow

Police used to ask drivers to breathe into a bag if they thought the driver had been drinking alcohol. The bag contained a red-orange chemical. This **reacted** with alcohol and turned green.

Luminol still glows if the blood is very old. It works even if the area has been cleaned.

Find Out More

American Chemical Society
The American Chemical Society has a division especially for school students. This provides teacher and student resources, competitions, a magazine, and a Web site.

Contact them at the following address:
American Chemical Society, 1155 Sixteenth Street, NW Washington, D.C., 20036

Books

Fullick, Ann. *Matter*. Chicago: Heinemann Library, 1999.

Oxlade, Chris. *Chemicals in Action: Material Changes and Reactions*. Chicago: Heinemann Library, 2002.

Snedden, Robert. *Material World: Changing Materials*. Chicago: Heinemann Library, 2001.

World Wide Web

To find out more about chemical reactions, you can search the Internet. Use keywords like these:

- fireworks
- crime +science
- reactions +catalysts
- chemicals +reactions

You can find your own keywords by using words from this book. The search tips on the next page will help you find useful Web sites.

Search tips

There are billions of pages on the Internet. It can be difficult to find exactly what you are looking for. These tips will help you find useful Web sites more quickly:

- Know what you want to find out about
- Use simple keywords
- Use two to six keywords in a search
- Only use names of people, places, or things
- Put double quote marks around words that go together, for example "neutralization reactions"

Where to search

Search engine

A search engine looks through millions of Web site pages. It lists all the sites that match the words in the search box. You will find the best matches are at the top of the list, on the first page.

Search directory

A person instead of a computer has sorted a search directory. You can search by keyword or subject and browse through the different sites. It is like looking through books on a library shelf.

Glossary

acid compound that has a sour taste and can burn you. Acids have a pH less than 7.

acid rain rain containing nitric acid and sulfuric acid

atom tiny particle that makes up everything

bacteria living things so small you need a microscope to see them

base chemical that neutralizes acids. Metal oxides and metal hydroxides are bases

carbonate compound that contains carbon, oxygen, and another element

catalyst material that speeds up a reaction without being used up

chemical property how a material will react when it is with other materials

chemical reaction change that produces one or more new materials

chemical symbol short way of writing the name of an element

compound material made of two or more different types of atoms

concentration amount of a material in a certain space

decomposer living thing that breaks apart compounds into simpler materials

decomposition reaction chemical reaction in which a compound breaks apart into simpler materials

diabetes condition in which there is too much sugar in the blood

digestion breakdown of food so that it can be used by the body

displace push out

displacement reaction chemical reaction in which one or more elements displace, or push out, another element in a compound

dissolve mix completely and evenly

electrolysis using electricity to break a compound apart

element material made from only one kind of atom

endothermic reaction reaction that takes in energy

energy ability to do work. Energy is transferred whenever something happens.

enzyme material that speeds up reactions in living things without being changed

exothermic reaction reaction that gives off energy, usually in the form of heat and light

fertilizer chemicals added to soils to help plants grow

formula symbols and numbers used to show how atoms are joined

fossil fuel fuel formed from the remains of plants and animals that lived millions of years ago; coal, oil, and gas are fossil fuels

fuel any material that can be burned to produce useful heat or power

glucose compound that is a type of sugar

hydroxide compound of a metal, hydrogen, and oxygen

inhibitor material that slows down a chemical reaction

intestine digestive canal between the stomach and the anus

lime calcium oxide or calcium hydroxide

mass amount of matter in an object

matter anything that takes up space and has mass

mixture material made of elements or compounds not joined chemically

molecule two or more atoms held together by chemical bonds

neutral neither an acid nor a base

neutralization reaction between an acid and a base to form a salt and water

oxidation reaction when a material joins up with oxygen

oxide compound formed when oxygen joins up with another element

particle tiny bit

photosynthesis reaction between carbon dioxide and water, using light energy, to form glucose and oxygen

physical change change in how something looks, not in what makes it up

physical property feature that can be seen or measured without changing what a material is made of

product material formed from a chemical reaction

property feature of something

react take part in a chemical reaction and produce one or more new materials

reactant material that reacts with another material during a chemical reaction

reaction rate measure of how fast a reaction happens

reactivity series materials listed by how easily they react with other materials

reduction reaction that happens when oxygen is removed from a material

respiration chemical reaction in which glucose and oxygen react to form carbon dioxide and water, releasing energy

saliva juice made in the mouth that contains an enzyme

salt material formed when an acid reacts with a base

soda ash sodium oxide

starch compound made of glucose units joined together

state of matter whether something is solid, liquid, or gas

surface area parts of a material that come in contact with a reactant

synthesis reaction chemical reaction in which two or more elements or compounds join to form one compound

vitamin chemical found in foods and needed for good health

water vapor water in a gas state

word equation chemical reaction described in words as an equation

yeast type of fungus used to make bread rise

Index